Seven Wonders of the
GAS GIANTS
AND THEIR MOONS

Ron Miller

TWENTY-FIRST CENTURY BOOKS

Minneapolis

Dedicated to Connor Lifson

PHOTO ACKNOWLEDGMENTS

The images in this book are used with the permission of: NASA/JPL, pp. 5, 9, 27, 75 (top left); NASA and The Hubble Heritage Team (STScI/AURA), p. 6; © Ron Miller/Black Cat Studios, pp. 7, 16, 18, 21, 24–25, 30, 31, 37, 38, 39, 41, 44, 51, 52, 56, 59, 62 (bottom), 64, 65, 66, 67, 69 (bottom right), 72, 75 (right center, bottom center); NASA/JPL/Space Science Institute, pp. 8, 11, 50, 53, 75 (top center, bottom left); © Imagno/Hulton Archive/Getty Images, p. 12 (top); Le opere di Galileo Galilei. Edizione nazionale sotto gli auspicii di Sua Maestà il re d'Italia (Vol. X, p. 410). Courtesy Woodson Research Center, Fondren Library, Rice University, p. 12 (bottom); NASA images courtesy of Black Cat Studios, pp. 13, 14–15, 15, 20, 23, 32, 34 (inset), 36, 47, 48, 49, 55 (top), 69 (top right, bottom left), 70 (both), 71 (right), NASA/CXC/M. Weiss, p. 19; © Science and Society/SuperStock, p. 22; NASA/ESA, p. 26; NASA/JPL/University of Arizona, pp. 28 (top), 33, 75 (bottom right and top right); © Thomas Jansson, p. 28 (bottom); © Bill Curtsinger/National Geographic/Getty Images, p. 34 (main); NASA/JPL/USGS, p. 40; © European Southern Observatory, p. 42; courtesy of History of Science Collections, University of Oklahoma Libraries, p. 45; NASA/JPL/ASU, p. 46; © Altrendo Travel/Getty Images, p. 54; NASA/JSC, p. 55 (bottom); NASA/JPL-Caltech/University of Arizona, p. 57 (left); NASA/GSFC Scientific Visualization Studio, p. 57 (right); X-ray: NASA/CXC/SwRI/R. Gladstone et al. Optical: NASA/ESA/Hubble Heritage (AURA/STcI), p. 58; © George Lepp/Stone/Getty Images, pp. 60–61; NASA, ESA, and Jonathan Nichols (University of Leicester), p. 62 (center); NASA, ESA, J. Clarke (Boston University), and Z. Levay (STScI), p. 62 (top); NASA/CXC/MSFC/R. Eisner et al., p. 63; Image created by Reto Stöckli, Nazmi El Saleous, and Marit Jentoft-Nilsen, NASA GSFC, p. 69 (top left); courtesy Olafur Ingolfsson, p. 71 (left); NASA/JPL-Caltech/University of Arizona/Texas A&M University, p. 73.

Front cover: NASA/JPL/Space Science Institute (top left and bottom left); © Ron Miller/Black Cat Studios (bottom center and bottom right); NASA/JPL/University of Arizona (top center and top right); NASA/JPL (center).

Twenty-First Century Books
A division of Lerner Publishing Group, Inc.
241 First Avenue North
Minneapolis, MN 55401 U.S.A.

Website address: www.lernerbooks.com

Library of Congress Cataloging-in-Publication Data

Miller, Ron, 1947–
    Seven wonders of the gas giants and their moons / Ron Miller.
        p.   cm. — (Seven wonders)
    Includes bibliographical references and index.
    ISBN 978–0–7613–5449–9 (lib. bdg. : alk. paper)
    1. Outer planets—Juvenile literature. I. Title.
    QB659.M55 2011
    523.4—dc22   2010015558

Manufactured in the United States of America
1 – DP – 12/31/10

Contents

INTRODUCTION

*P*EOPLE LOVE TO MAKE LISTS OF THE BIGGEST AND THE BEST. ALMOST TWENTY-FIVE HUNDRED YEARS AGO, A GREEK WRITER NAMED HERODOTUS MADE A LIST OF THE MOST AWESOME THINGS EVER BUILT BY PEOPLE. THE LIST INCLUDED BUILDINGS, STATUES, AND OTHER OBJECTS THAT WERE LARGE, WONDROUS, AND IMPRESSIVE. LATER, OTHER WRITERS ADDED NEW ITEMS TO THE LIST. WRITERS EVENTUALLY AGREED ON A FINAL LIST. IT WAS CALLED THE SEVEN WONDERS OF THE ANCIENT WORLD.

The list became so famous that people began imitating it. They made other lists of wonders. They listed the Seven Wonders of the Modern World and the Seven Wonders of the Medieval World. People even made lists of undersea wonders and the wonders of science and technology.

But Earth doesn't contain all the wonders that have been discovered. Our planet shares the solar system with many other worlds. They all have wonderful things to see. Not the least of these are the wonders of the gas giants and their amazing moons.

WHAT ARE THE GAS GIANTS?

Our solar system has three kinds of planets. There are rocky planets such as Earth, Venus, Mars, and Mercury. Then there are small icy worlds such as the dwarf planet Pluto. The other kinds are gas giant planets. These are

This illustration brings together images of the four gas giants taken by the Voyager *spacecraft in the late 1970s and 1980s. The gas giants are* (from left) *Uranus, Neptune, Saturn, and Jupiter. They are shown roughly to scale with each other.*

Jupiter, Saturn, Uranus, and Neptune. The gas giants are made mostly of gas and liquid. Hydrogen and helium are the main ingredients. But there are other gases, as well, such as ammonia, methane, and even water vapor.

The gas giants are very large planets. Jupiter is twice as large as all the other planets combined. Even Neptune, the smallest, is seventeen times as large as Earth.

All the gas giants have large numbers of moons. At last count, Jupiter has at least sixty-three moons and Saturn at least thirty-four. Some of these moons are almost as large as some of the rocky planets and icy worlds. The largest of these moons, Jupiter's Ganymede, is nearly as big as Mercury. Since it's always a lot more fun to visit a wonder than just hear about it, let's start our journey.

1 Saturn's Rings

This series of images of Saturn was taken over four years by a telescope orbiting Earth.

$\mathcal{S}$ATURN WOULD LOOK LIKE A SMALLER VERSION OF JUPITER IF NOT FOR ONE THING—ITS MYSTERIOUS RINGS. THEY SURROUND SATURN LIKE AN ENORMOUS FLAT WHITE DISK. THERE IS NOTHING IN THE SOLAR SYSTEM QUITE LIKE THEM. THE RINGS CAN BE EASILY SEEN THROUGH EVEN A SMALL TELESCOPE. WHEN THEY ARE TILTED TOWARD OR AWAY FROM EARTH, THE RINGS ARE A MAGNIFICENT SIGHT. THEY APPEAR BRILLIANT WHITE AGAINST THE PALE YELLOW PLANET. BUT SOMETIMES THE PLANET IS TIPPED SO THE RINGS ARE SEEN EDGE ON. WHEN THIS HAPPENS, THEY ALMOST DISAPPEAR.

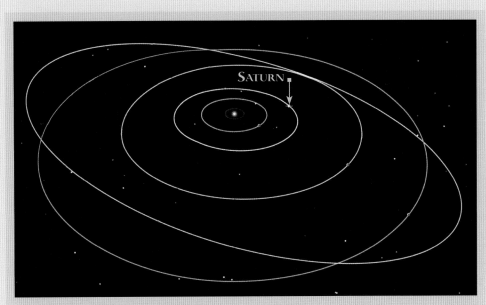

Saturn's orbit around the Sun is in yellow.

The rings of Saturn are vast when viewed from the top, but viewed from the side, the rings are barely visible.

The rings are unbelievably vast. They cover an area of more than 15 billion square miles (40 billion square kilometers). That is eighty times the total surface area of Earth. To travel from the inner edge of the rings to the outer edge, a space traveler would have to cover a distance equal to thirteen trips across the United States. The rings' full width from one side to the other is 70 percent that of the distance between Earth and the Moon. The thickness of the rings, however, only rarely exceeds 33 feet (10 meters). They each probably average only 6 feet (2 m) in thickness.

The rings are divided into three distinct bands—the outer band; the A ring; and the broader, brighter B ring. Separating them is the Cassini Division. It appears to be narrow because the rings are so large. The Cassini Division is actually big enough to drop the Moon through! Inside the B ring is the dim, transparent crepe ring (also called the C ring). Images from spacecraft have shown at least seven distinct major rings. The A and B rings are themselves made up of five hundred to one thousand extremely narrow rings, like the grooves on an old-fashioned phonograph record.

The rings are made of billions of chunks of nearly pure water ice, something like the ice cubes you buy in a bag at a convenience store. Some of the chunks may be "dirty," or coated with dust. A few of the chunks may

MOONS AND *Planets*

What is the difference between a moon and a planet? A planet is a spherical body, such as Earth or Jupiter, that orbits (circles) a star, such as the Sun. A planet gives off no light of its own—it can be seen only by the light it reflects from its sun. A moon orbits a planet. Astronomers call them *satellites* (which means "companions"). Our moon is the satellite of Earth. Callisto, Io, Europa, and Ganymede are all satellites of Jupiter. Sometimes they are called natural satellites to distinguish them from artificial ones such as the Hubble Space Telescope or the International Space Station.

be 0.5 miles (1 km) wide. But most are very small particles. They probably range in size from grains of sugar to basketballs. As big as the rings are, they don't contain much material. If all the ice in the rings was squeezed together, it would form a ball only 60 miles (100 km) across. Each of these ring particles, no matter how small, is an individual moon. It circles Saturn in its own orbit. So it can be said that Saturn is a planet with a billion moons!

The colors in this image represent the sizes of the particles in Saturn's rings. Purple regions have particles less than 2 inches (5 centimeters) in diameter. Green and blue regions have particles of less than 0.3 inches (1 cm). The white band has particles packed too close together to get an accurate reading of the particle size. The Cassini Division is the black band to the right of the white area.

About Saturn

Saturn is a big planet. It is the second largest in the solar system. It is nine and one-half times wider than Earth and thirty times bigger around. If Saturn's equator (an imaginary line around its middle) were a belt that could be unfastened and stretched out straight, it would reach 240,000 miles (386,000 km). That's the distance of Earth to the Moon. Eighty Earths could be flattened out and spread over Saturn's surface. More than seven hundred planets Earth's size could be packed inside it.

Usually, the larger a planet or other body is, the greater its mass. (Mass is the amount of stuff a body is made of.) But for all of its size, Saturn has the least mass of all the planets. This is because Saturn is made mostly of very light elements, such as hydrogen and helium. When a planet has little mass, its surface gravity is weak. So even though Saturn is much larger than Earth, a person would only weigh slightly more there than on Earth. A 150-pound (68-kilogram) person would weigh 160.5 pounds (73 kg) on Saturn.

All the gas giant planets rotate very quickly. Saturn rotates so rapidly that its day is only 10 hours and 39.4 minutes long. The force created by Saturn's rapid spin makes it bulge at its equator. Seen through a telescope, Saturn does not look perfectly round, as Earth's Moon does. Instead, it seems slightly squashed.

Astronomers believe that Saturn has a huge, molten rocky core about the size of Earth. Above this is a thick layer of metallic hydrogen. Hydrogen is the lightest element. On Earth hydrogen is usually a light gas. It was

Gravity

Gravity is a force created by mass. The more mass an object has, the more gravity it produces. Just because something is big doesn't mean it has a lot of mass. Mass is a measure of how much material is crammed into a given space. A balloon is bigger than a baseball, but it has less mass. This is because the atoms of air in the balloon are not as closely packed together as the atoms inside the ball.

Earth has nearly 6 trillion tons (5.4 trillion metric tons) of mass. It takes all of this mass to create enough gravity to make you weigh what you do. When you stand on a scale, you are measuring the amount of force by which Earth is attracting you. Because you have mass too, you are also attracting Earth!

SATURN
Facts

Distance from the Sun:
   888.2 million miles
   (1.4 billion km)
Diameter: 75,000 miles
   (120,536 km)
Length of year: 29.42 years
**Length of day: 10 hours 40
   minutes**

once used to fill balloons and dirigibles (airships). But the pressure deep below the surface of Saturn is tremendous. It has compressed the gas so much that it has turned into a metal-like substance.

Above the metallic hydrogen is a layer of liquid hydrogen. Above that is a deep gaseous atmosphere. This atmosphere is mostly hydrogen gas with a little helium and a few other elements. These gases can combine to form many compounds, such as methane, propane, acetylene, and ammonia. When these compounds freeze or liquefy, they make the brightly colored clouds seen from Earth.

Saturn is completely covered by clouds. No one has ever seen what lies beneath them. Seen from space, Saturn's clouds are complex swirling patterns. The patterns are stretched by the planet's rapid rotation into long streaks and bands. Saturn produces more heat from within itself than it receives from the faraway Sun. That heat rising from deep inside the planet causes huge storms on the surface. The swirling cloud patterns are actually cyclonic storms, like

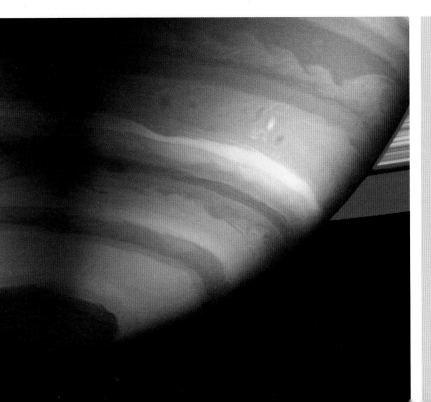

The bright orange lines in this close-up of Saturn are the clouds of a powerful storm known as the Dragon Storm.

hurricanes on Earth. The winds of these storms are among the most ferocious in the solar system. They blow at speeds of up to 1,060 miles (1,700 km) an hour. This is faster than the speed of sound!

DISCOVERING THE RINGS

The Italian scientist Galileo Galilei first saw Saturn's rings in 1610. He had no idea what they could be. His homemade telescope was small and not very powerful. It was not even as good as a modern pair of binoculars. He could not quite see Saturn well enough to make out any details. All he could tell was that there was something very strange about the planet. "When I observe Saturn," Galileo wrote, "the central star appears the largest; two others, one situated to the east, the other to the west. . . seem to touch it. They are like two servants who help old Saturn on his way, and always remain at his side."

In 1655 twenty-six-year-old Dutch astronomer Christiaan Huygens observed Saturn with a much better telescope than Galileo's. He discovered three important facts about Saturn. He learned that Saturn is surrounded by a flat ring and that the ring does not touch the planet. He also noted that the ring is tipped compared to Earth's orbit. This tip is called the ecliptic.

In 1675 Giovanni Domenico Cassini—an Italian astronomer who had moved to France to work at the new Paris Observatory—observed something new. He realized that the ring was actually two rings divided by a gap. Soon other astronomers discovered additional gaps in the rings.

Galileo Galilei (top) drew this image (above) of Saturn in his notebook. His telescope was not powerful enough for him to accurately make out the rings.

THE GAPS in the Ring

Dark gaps separate Saturn's rings. Two of these gaps are visible from Earth with even small telescopes. But spacecraft have discovered that there are hundreds of gaps. The big gaps are caused by the large inner moons of Saturn. Their gravity pulls on the ring particles. As a moon orbits, the particles at a certain distance get pulled on more often than the rest. Every time a moon lines up with a particle, it gives it a little nudge. This eventually forms an empty space in the ring. Each of Saturn's large moons—Titan, Rhea, and Mimas—orbiting outside the rings has its own gap. Other gaps are caused by tiny moons—called shepherd moons—orbiting within the rings *(below)*. And other gaps are similar to the ripples caused when a stone is tossed into a pool of water.

WHAT ARE THE RINGS?

The earliest observers of Saturn didn't know what to make of the rings. Most assumed that they were solid, like a disk cut from a sheet of paper. Cassini suggested that the rings were formed of a swarm of millions of individual particles of matter. But this idea was pretty much ignored. In 1795 the French mathematician Pierre-Simon Laplace calculated that a solid ring was impossible. It would be broken up by Saturn's gravity.

In 1850 William C. Bond and George P. Bond of the United States and William Rutter Dawes of Britain discovered an entirely new ring inside the two previously known ones. They called this ring the crepe ring because it is so thin and transparent that it resembles crepe paper. Some astronomers suggested that the rings were some sort of liquid, while others thought they might be made of gas.

WHERE DID THE RINGS COME FROM?

In 1848 French mathematician Edouard Roche calculated what would happen if a large natural satellite (such as a moon) approached too close to a large planet. Roche said the satellite would be torn apart by

This image is a natural color mosaic of the rings of Saturn.

the gravitational forces of the planet. This happens because the gravitational attraction of a planet on a moon is not equal all the way around. The planet pulls more on the side of the moon closest to it and less on the side farther away. If the moon gets too close, this unequal pull can become great enough to tear the moon apart. Every planet has what is called a Roche limit. Very tiny satellites can orbit unharmed within the Roche limit. They are too small for the difference in the pull of gravity between one side and another to break them up. But if a large satellite comes within the Roche limit, it will be pulled into pieces.

Saturn's rings lay within the Roche limit of the planet. Astronomers realized the rings might have formed when a satellite wandered too close to Saturn and was destroyed. Its particles began orbiting the planet in bands. Those individual particles give the appearance of a solid ring when seen from a distance.

Other astronomers believe that the rings are material that was unable to form into a moon because it lay within Saturn's Roche limit. Within this distance, the gravitational pull of a planet prevents particles from clumping together to form a moon. Another idea suggests that during the time when Saturn was first forming, it had one or more moons just outside its Roche limit. The bigger a planet is, the more gravity it has. And the more gravity it has, the bigger its Roche limit is. So as Saturn grew larger, its Roche limit grew too. The limit eventually

"The scientific theory I like best is that the rings of Saturn are composed entirely of lost airline luggage."
—*American comedian Mark Russell, 2009*

DIFFERENT
Origins

Recent discoveries suggest that not all of Saturn's rings were created the same way. Saturn's outermost ring is very thin. It is almost invisible from Earth. One of Saturn's innermost moons, Enceladus, has giant geysers (on Earth these are hot springs that erupt steam and boiling water). These throw vast amounts of material—mostly water ice—into space. This ice would be in the form of extremely tiny particles, like miniature snowflakes or sleet. These icy particles have spiraled down toward Saturn, forming a thin, almost invisible ring beyond the A ring.

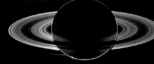

moved past the inner moons. These moons soon broke apart. The remnants of the destroyed moons spread out to form the magnificent rings. There may still be large pieces of these ancient moons within the rings. They would be much smaller than their ancestors but a thousand times larger than a typical ring particle.

Another theory suggests that a few hundred million years ago—at a time when the early ancestors of the dinosaurs were roaming Earth—Saturn may have had no rings at all. The rings formed when one or more small moons wandered too close to Saturn. When they got within the Roche limit, Saturn's gravity pulled them apart. After millions of years of bumping against one another, the pieces of moon were ground into the tiny particles that form the rings today.

This illustration shows what Saturn's rings look like close up. They are made up of small bits of space debris.

EXPLORING THE RINGS

Only three spacecraft have visited Saturn. Two of them, *Voyager 1* arrived in 1980 and *Voyager 2* in 1981. These spacecraft flew past the planet, so their visits were very short. Nevertheless, the few pictures sent back to Earth showed many surprising details. For example, Saturn has a very narrow outer ring, named the F ring. It looks as if parts of this ring are braided. Other photos showed what looked like giant, shadowy "spokes" on the rings. The *Cassini* spacecraft has been orbiting Saturn since 2004. It has sent tens of thousands of pictures back to Earth. These have shown the rings to be extremely complex, ever-changing structures.

"It's been an adventure just getting out to Saturn. . . . It's a joy, really, to be able to take our images and composite [merge] them in an artful way. . . . It's about poetry and beauty and science all mixed together."

—*Carolyn Porco, head of the* Cassini *mission imaging science team, 2005*

> *"The studies we're doing at Saturn go well beyond the understanding of ring systems. It could tell us a lot about how planets form around other stars."*
>
> —*Edward Weiler, National Aeronautics and Space Administration (NASA) associate administrator for space science, 2004*

Cassini also discovered that the tiny moons orbiting in the rings create a wake, in much the same way that a boat creates a wake when moving through water. These wakes cause the rings to ripple and wave as the moons move among them.

Understanding how Saturn's rings formed and how they work help provide clues on how our solar system—and Earth—formed. Many stars are surrounded by broad, flat dust disks. These are very much like Saturn's rings, though many, many times larger. Scientists believe that these dust disks are solar systems in their early stages of forming. Our own solar system may have begun from a similar disk of dust that once circled the Sun. Understanding how Saturn's rings work gives scientists valuable firsthand knowledge. They are learning how these rings form and what happens inside them. Observing Saturn's rings is like looking 4 billion years into the solar system's past.

MYSTERIES OF THE RINGS

There are still many things about Saturn's rings that scientists don't understand. And as new data arrives from spacecraft, new mysteries are created. The rings seem to have an atmosphere. It is made mostly of oxygen, like Earth's atmosphere, but it is much too thin to breathe. No one knows where this atmosphere comes from or what keeps it in place. Scientists have detected iron and other elements within the icy rings. They don't know yet where this material came from either. And the strange, dark "spokes" photographed during the *Voyager* mission are still puzzling astronomers. They may be the result of some unknown electrical activity. *Cassini* spacecraft photos have also shown that the material in the rings is not distributed smoothly. There are mysterious clumps and patches where particles seem to have clung together.

As *Cassini* sends more and more information, Saturn's rings are shown to be more beautiful than anyone had ever thought—and stranger than anyone had ever dreamed.

This illustration displays the beauty of Saturn's rings as they would look from Saturn's surface.

OTHER RINGED PLANETS

Saturn is not the only planet with rings. All the gas giant planets have them. But they are all very different from Saturn's magnificent rings.

Jupiter has a ring, but it is almost invisible. No one even suspected that it was there until one of the Voyager mission spacecraft sped past in 1979. As it did, the craft took a photo looking back at the planet. With the Sun behind it, the almost invisible ring was illuminated in a dim, ghostly glow. Saturn's rings are made of large particles of ice. Jupiter's ring is made of dark dust. The particles that make up the ring are about as tiny as those in a puff of smoke.

The rings around Uranus are also made of dark dust. They are almost as dark as charcoal. Instead of a broad, flat disk like Jupiter's ring, however, the rings of Uranus are narrow bands. They look like loops of string around the planet. Tiny moons orbiting between the loops keep the spaces empty of dust.

The rings of Neptune are even more unique. Like the rings around Uranus, they are dark, narrow bands. But the rings are formed of pieces, as though someone had cut out portions of them. These ring segments are very mysterious, and so far, no one is sure how they formed.

2 THE GREAT RED SPOT of Jupiter

Jupiter is the largest planet in the solar system.

$\mathcal{J}$UPITER IS A PLANET OF STORMS. VAST HURRICANES RAGE THROUGH ITS ATMOSPHERE. THE LARGEST OF THESE HURRICANES IS SO ENORMOUS THAT IT IS VISIBLE FROM EARTH. IT WAS FIRST SEEN IN THE SEVENTEENTH CENTURY, WHEN IT WAS NAMED THE GREAT RED SPOT. THE HURRICANE'S SWIRLING CLOUDS COVER AN OVAL 7,500 MILES (12,000 KM) WIDE AND 1,500 MILES (25,000 KM) LONG. THIS IS TWICE THE SIZE OF EARTH.

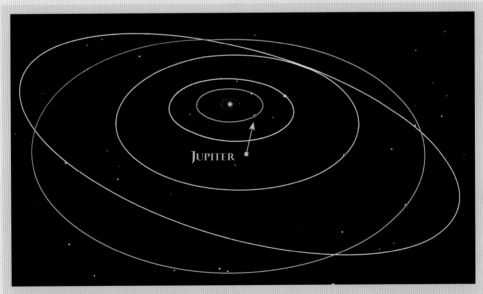

Jupiter, the innermost of the gas planets, orbits well beyond Mars, the outermost rocky planet.

Like a hurricane on Earth, the Great Red Spot spins. But where a hurricane rotates once in just a few hours, the Great Red Spot is so large it takes six days to make one rotation. The size and appearance of the Great Red Spot varies from time to time. Some years, it nearly faded from view. In the 1880s, it was twice as large as it is at present.

Early observers didn't know what to make of the Great Red Spot. Associating its color with heat, some people suggested that it might be a

This drawing of Jupiter by a French astronomer in the 1880s shows the Great Red Spot.

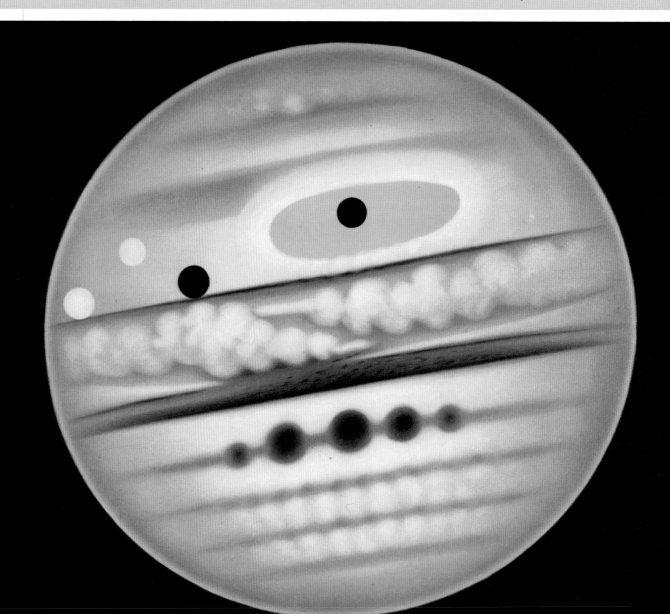

gigantic volcano. Another theory held that it was a huge island floating in Jupiter's sea of clouds. Modern astronomers know that the Great Red Spot is a vast storm system. But how can a storm be so large, let alone last for four hundred years? The answer is that Jupiter does not depend on the Sun to drive its weather.

A hurricane or cyclone on Earth gets its energy from Sun-warmed oceans. When the storm moves over cooler water or land, its source of energy is gone, and it disappears. The temperature changes caused by Earth's seasons also help to create and break up storm systems. But Jupiter creates its own heat.

It does this because it is so large. The larger a planet is, the more gravity it has. And the more gravity it has, the harder it pulls on the material of which it is made. Jupiter has so much gravity that the material near its center is squeezed very tightly. As this material is squeezed, it grows hot. You can see how this works by rapidly squeezing a rubber ball in your hand. You will feel the ball grow very warm. The same thing happens inside Jupiter.

"The ingenious Dr. [Robert] Hooke did some months since [tell] a friend of his that he had . . . observed . . . a spot in the largest of the observed belts of Jupiter."
—Philosophical Transactions of the Royal Society, *an organization of British scientists, 1664*

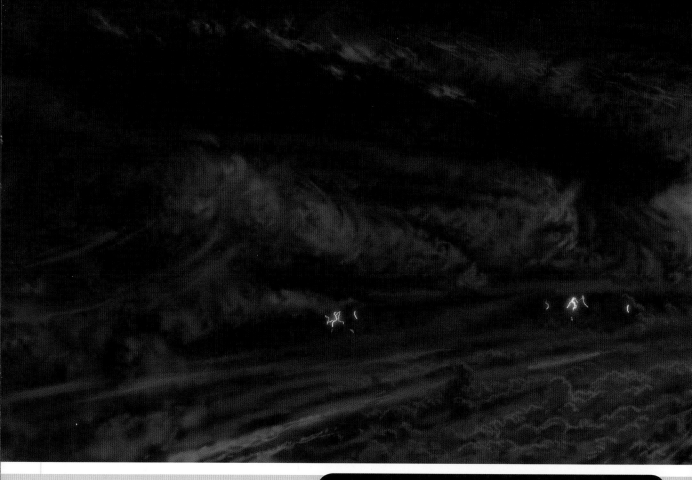

As long as Jupiter's energy source continues, there is nothing to keep a storm from stopping once it has started. Jupiter does not have any landmasses to break up storms—the surface of the planet is pretty much the same all over. Nor does it have any seasons. These are two things that help control weather on Earth.

In addition to the Great Red Spot, smaller cyclones come and go constantly. They often look like small white ovals when seen from space. Occasionally they

Seasons

Seasons are caused by the tilt of a planet's axis of rotation. A planet whose axis is level is said to have 0 degrees tilt. The axes of most of the planets in the solar system are tilted, however. Earth's axis is tilted about 23 degrees, but Jupiter is tilted only 3 degrees. A tilted axis causes the amount of sunlight reaching different parts of the surface of the planet to change during the course of a year. The more an axis is tilted, the more extreme the seasons are. The 3-degree tilt of Jupiter's axis means that the sunlight Jupiter receives is nearly constant year-round. The temperature changes very little during the year.

This illustration visualizes the Great Red Spot from just outside the storm in the atmosphere of Jupiter.

collide with the Great Red Spot. The Great Red Spot absorbs them, like debris swirling down a drain.

ABOUT JUPITER

Everything about Jupiter is really big. It is eleven times the diameter of Earth. It would take 300 planets as big as Earth to balance Jupiter on a scale. More than 1,330 planets the size of our own would be needed to fill a hollow sphere the size of Jupiter. It is more than twice as massive as all the other planets combined. It is second only to the Sun in size. As one astronomer put it, the solar system could be rightly described as consisting of only the Sun, Jupiter, and debris. It is no wonder that Jupiter was named after the king of the ancient Roman gods.

Jupiter rotates very fast—much faster than Earth does. Its day is only a little over ten hours long. This is less than half that of an Earth day. Someone standing on the equator of Earth is moving at about 1,000 miles (1,600 km) an hour. But someone standing on Jupiter's equator would be moving at 27,900 miles (44,897 km) an hour! This rapid rotation has an effect on Jupiter's weather. It is the reason why Jupiter's colorful clouds are stretched into long ribbons around the planet.

The gas that composes most of Jupiter's bulk is hydrogen. Hydrogen is a very light element. So Jupiter is much larger than Earth, yet it has only two and one-half times Earth's gravity.

The colorful bands encircling Jupiter are clouds stretched into thin streams.

The Great Dark Spot of Neptune visible at the center of this image had disappeared by 1994.

Scooter

Voyager 2 discovered another storm south of Neptune's Great Dark Spot. Although it was much smaller, it moved a lot faster. Astronomers nicknamed it Scooter. Like its bigger cousin, it was blue, but it had a core of bright white clouds. The Great Dark Spot was not as permanent as the Great Red Spot on Jupiter. When the Hubble Space Telescope photographed Neptune in 1994, the spot was gone. Instead, a new blue spot had appeared in the northern hemisphere.

NEPTUNE'S DARK SPOT

Jupiter is not the only gas giant planet to have huge storms. When *Voyager 2* flew past Neptune in 1989, it discovered an enormous blue oval in its southern hemisphere. Sometimes also called the Great Dark Spot, this was a vast storm similar to Jupiter's Great Red Spot. It was nearly 8,000 miles (12,500 km) wide. This is as wide as the entire Earth. The spot rotated like hurricanes on Earth, with winds blowing as fast as 700 miles (1,124 km) an hour.

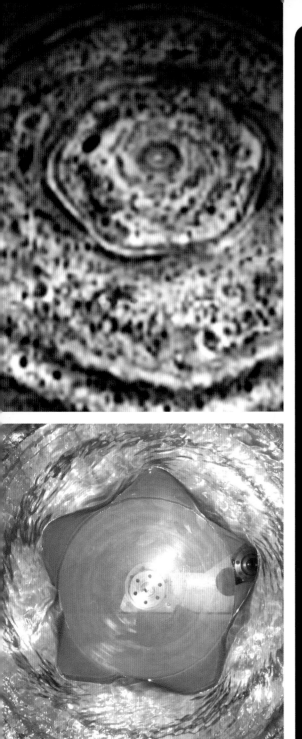

THE MYSTERIOUS *Hexagon*

Saturn, too, has many giant storms, although none are as large or long lasting as those on Jupiter or Neptune. But Saturn has something just as impressive as Jupiter's Great Red Spot. It is related to the spots on Jupiter and Neptune because it is a cloud pattern caused by weather. What makes it unique is its shape. Surrounding the north pole of Saturn is a gigantic hexagon. The six-sided shape is nearly 15,000 miles (24,000 km) across. It was first seen by the *Voyager* spacecraft in 1983, so it must be a very long-lasting feature. Scientists were puzzled about how this hexagon formed and how it keeps its shape.

In 2006 a scientist named Tomas Bohr performed some experiments with rotating liquids. He used a liquid because liquids in motion act just like gases in an atmosphere—but are much easier to handle and study. Bohr dropped a fluid similar to water onto a rotating round plate. If the speed of the plate was just right, the outline of the fluid would form into one of several shapes. A hexagon, like that on Saturn, was one of them.

Bohr's experiment shows that the feature is a perfectly natural one, even if we don't know yet how it forms. Since Earth is also a rotating sphere like Saturn, with fluid oceans and atmosphere, these discoveries may eventually help us learn how Earth's weather works.

Top: *The north pole of Saturn features this six-sided pattern.*
Bottom: *Scientist Tomas Bohr showed that liquids could form into shapes (such as this five-sided figure) when they are rotated at certain speeds.*

Of the four gas giant planets in our solar system, Neptune is the farthest away. It is 3 billion miles (4.5 billion km) from the Sun. It takes 164 years for Neptune to orbit the Sun just once. This means it has just made one full orbit since it was discovered in 1846.

Neptune is large enough to hold nearly sixty planets the size of Earth. Its atmosphere is made mostly of hydrogen, with some helium and a little methane. The dark blue methane clouds—including the Great Dark Spot—form the planet's main cloud deck. As high as 30 to 45 miles (50 to 75 km) above the methane clouds are white, wispy clouds. They are probably made of water ice crystals. Neptune's day is only sixteen hours long. Because of this rapid rotation, wind speeds can reach more than 1,300 miles (2,100 km) an hour. The winds stretch most of the high white clouds into long, straight bands.

NEPTUNE'S OWN HEAT

What powers Neptune's storms? Heat from the Sun provides the energy for Earth's weather. But the Sun is thirty times smaller in Neptune's sky than it is in Earth's. This means that it provides only 1/900 the light and heat. Like Jupiter, gravitational pull deep within Neptune provides more heat than it receives from the Sun. But Neptune radiates much more heat than Jupiter does—almost three times more than it receives from the Sun as compared to Jupiter's two and a half times. If the Sun were to suddenly go out, Neptune would hardly notice.

There is a lot of amazing weather on many of the planets. Some of them have storms that make a hurricane on Earth look like a gentle breeze. But nothing beats the Great Red Spot of Jupiter for power and wonder!

3 THE *Volcanoes* OF IO

This illustration shows what volcanoes erupting on the surface of Io, one of Jupiter's moons, might look like.

$\mathcal{E}$ARTH HAS MORE THAN SIX HUNDRED ACTIVE VOLCANOES. OTHER WORLDS IN THE SOLAR SYSTEM HAVE VOLCANOES TOO. MANY OF THESE VOLCANOES DWARF ANYTHING EARTH CAN OFFER. YET, THE MOST VOLCANICALLY ACTIVE PLACE IN THE SOLAR SYSTEM IS NOT A PLANET. IT'S A MOON.

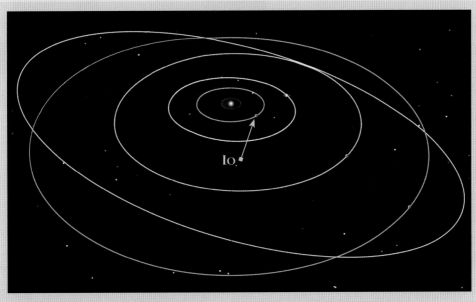

Io is one of the moons of Jupiter. It orbits Jupiter while that planet orbits the Sun.

Io is one of the four large moons of Jupiter known as the Galilean satellites. They were named after Italian scientist Galileo Galilei. He first saw the moons in 1610. The moons are Io, Europa, Callisto, and Ganymede. All but Europa are bigger than Earth's Moon. Io, which is just a bit larger than Earth's Moon, orbits 262,000 miles (421,600 km) from Jupiter. This is about the same distance the Moon is from Earth. Jupiter is so big, though, it fills Io's sky like an enormous striped balloon. If you were to replace the Moon with Jupiter, it would be forty times larger in our sky than a full Moon. Because Io, like the Moon, keeps one side always facing its planet, Jupiter never rises or sets there.

Galileo first discovered the four largest moons of Jupiter in the 1600s. They are (clockwise from top left) Ganymede, Callisto, Europa, and Io.

DISCOVERING THE VOLCANOES

On March 18, 1979, scientist Linda Morabito was examining one of the latest photos of Io sent back by the *Voyager 1* spacecraft. She noticed something strange in the picture. There appeared to be a large crescent-shaped cloud extending past the edge of the moon. But since Io has no atmosphere, a cloud would be impossible. She thought it might be part of another moon peeking past the other side of Io. This, too, was impossible. There was no moon on the other side of Io—certainly not one as large as this one would have to be.

Io *Facts*

Distance from Jupiter: 261,970 miles (421,600 km)
Diameter: 2,256 miles (3,630 km)
Length of time to orbit Jupiter: 1.77 days

The only thing it could possibly be was a huge, ongoing volcanic eruption. The next day, other scientists found several more volcanic plumes. If volcanoes were erupting on Io, this would also explain a bright spot visible on its dark side. It was light from molten lava—melted rock and minerals. These were the first active volcanoes to ever be discovered on a world other than Earth.

At first glance, Io resembles a cheese pizza. It has blotchy, swirling patterns of red, yellow, orange, and white. Or perhaps it looks like something left sitting in the refrigerator too long. Most of the other moons in the solar system are

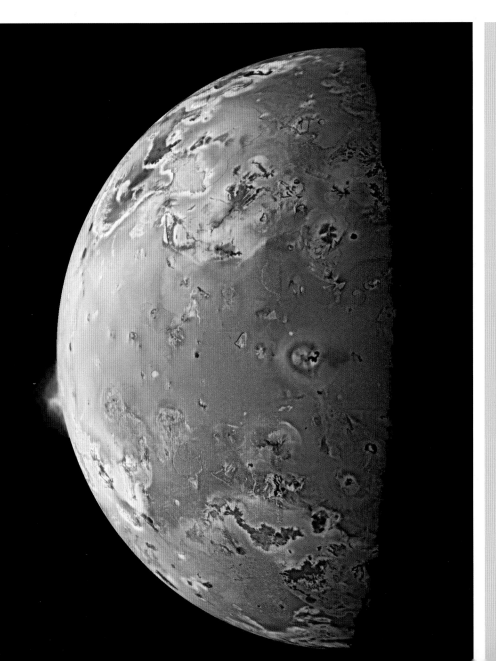

Volcanic plumes are visible in this image of Io. One is on the edge of the planet at left. The other is in the center of the image. It is a white circle with a dark circle and another white circle around it.

"I happened to catch one color image of Io that showed this unusual heartshaped feature on the surface. It was so remarkable it was almost shocking. I had expected yet another dead, cratered moon, and yet this seemed alive. It moved me deeply and it's something I remember vividly."

—Linda Morabito Kelly, planetary scientist, 2002

covered with craters. These were caused by the impact of meteors (small chunks of rock and metal). Instead of meteor craters, Io's surface features hundreds of volcanic calderas, or large flat-floored depressions caused by volcanoes.

Many volcanoes have huge pools of lava beneath them. These pools are called lava chambers. If an eruption empties this pool quickly, the mountain above will collapse into the empty chamber. This creates a caldera. The Hawaiian volcano Mauna Loa is a caldera.

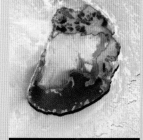

Below: *Mauna Loa, a volcano in Hawaii, erupts at night.*
Insert: *The visible color* (top right) *and infrared (heat) images* (bottom right) *show the hot and cool spots of a caldera (crater) on Io's surface. The eruptions of volcanoes on Io look much different from those on Earth.*

Many of the calderas on Io are violently active. In fact, more volcanoes are erupting at any one time on Io than on Earth. This makes Io the most volcanically active body in the solar system. New eruptions break out all the time. Some of the most powerful eruptions throw bright plumes of material up to 186 miles (300 km) above the surface. These eruptions look nothing like the volcanoes we see on our planet. Since Io has very little atmosphere, the dust and gas do not create the billowing clouds we see spewing from volcanoes on Earth. Instead, Io's volcanoes look like vast garden sprinklers. The gas and dust curve in huge arcs, forming umbrella-shaped plumes over the vents, or cracks in the planet's surface.

TUG OF WAR

As a moon orbits a planet, the planet's gravity pulls hardest on the side of the moon that is closest to it. The pull of gravity is weaker on the far side of the moon. This is because the force of gravity grows weaker with distance. This uneven pull is called a tide. Tides can cause a moon to flex like a rubber ball. If this flexing is strong enough, it can generate great amounts of heat. (It can even tear apart a moon that orbits too closely.) Bend a paper clip back and forth until it breaks, and then feel the ends of the broken pieces. They will feel warm. In the same way, the flexing of a moon by tides will cause it to grow warmer.

Io is caught in a kind of tug-of-war between Jupiter and the planet's large moons Europa and Callisto. Each time the moons pass close to Io, they pull it in the opposite direction from Jupiter. This causes additional stresses within Io's crust (surface layer). These forces cause the surface of Io to rise and fall by as much as 300 feet (90 m) during the forty-three hours it takes the moon to make a single orbit of Jupiter! This movement creates a huge amount of friction within the crust of the moon. This friction generates vast amounts of heat. It is enough heat to melt the interior of Io. As this melted material reaches the surface, it creates Io's volcanoes.

"[Discovering the volcano on Io] was a moment that every astronomer, every planetary scientist lives for."
—Linda Morabito Kelly, planetary scientist, 2002

Some of Io's volcanoes spew molten rock, like volcanoes on Earth do. Others erupt molten sulfur compounds. Sulfur changes color depending on its temperature. This sulfur gives Io its extraordinary colors.

It would be almost impossible to chart a map of Io. The eruptions and flowing sulfur are constantly changing the surface of this moon. New material flows onto the surface at a rate of about 0.4 inches (1 centimeter) a year. About 0.5 miles (1 km) is added to the surface of Io every one hundred thousand years.

MORE PLANETARY VOLCANOES

Many other worlds in the solar system have volcanoes—what astronomers call geothermal features. This means features that are driven by underground heat. Earth is one of these volcanic worlds, of course. But there are at least two and maybe three others.

The planet Neptune has one giant moon, named Triton. It is 1,680 miles (2,700 km) in diameter, only slightly smaller than Earth's Moon. The temperature on the surface of Triton is −391°F (−235°C). One reason Triton is so cold is that its surface is very bright. This means that it reflects most of the heat it gets from the Sun. At this

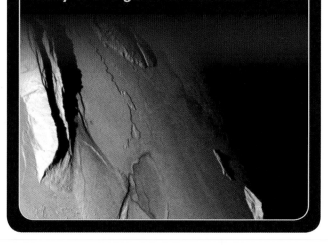

THE MYSTERIOUS MOUNTAINS *of Io*

Io has huge mountains *(below)*. One called Euboea Montes is 8 miles (13 km) high. This is higher than the tallest mountain on Earth. Astronomers are not certain how Io's mountains formed. One cause might be the new material that is being constantly added to the surface by the volcanoes. The weight of this material presses down on the surface crust. The crust cracks under the weight and forms large blocks. As one part of a block is pressed down, another part will be pushed up. It is like pressing down on one end of a piece of floating wood. As one end sinks, the other will rise. This process may be what creates many of Io's giant mountains.

temperature, methane, nitrogen, and carbon dioxide are frozen solid.

When the *Voyager 2* spacecraft flew past Triton in 1989, it photographed several dark plumes rising above the surface. Some of them rose as high as 5 miles (8 km) into the sky. These turned out to be ice volcanoes. These volcanoes do not erupt molten rock the way Earth volcanoes do or molten sulfur as on Io. Instead, Triton's volcanoes erupt liquid nitrogen, methane, and dust. Because these volcanoes are very cold, astronomers call them cryovolcanoes, or cryogeysers. (*Cryo* means "cold.") Scientists aren't too sure what powers them. It may be heat generated by Neptune's gravitational pull on Triton, as Jupiter heats Io. Even though Triton has a cold surface, its interior is still hot enough to cause eruptions.

A geyser on Triton spews nitrogen, methane, and dust. Neptune looms in the background of the illustration.

This illustration shows a cryogeyser ejecting water ice on Enceladus, one of Saturn's moons. Saturn is silhouetted by the Sun at left.

Another moon in the solar system also has cryogeysers. This is a small moon of Saturn, called Enceladus. This moon is only 310 miles (500 km) wide. Many astronomers had thought that Enceladus was much too small to have volcanic features. Others, though, thought it might be possible. Enceladus orbits close enough to Saturn for Saturn's gravity to heat its interior.

These scientists were proven right in 2005. That year the *Cassini* spacecraft discovered giant cryogeysers on Enceladus. The spacecraft photographed vast feathery plumes spraying from vents near the south pole. The geysers are very powerful. The material leaves the vents at hundreds of miles an hour. It can shoot as far as 200 miles (300 km) above the surface. To see one close up would be like looking at a huge rocket engine. Most of the material being ejected is water ice. This leads scientists to believe that Enceladus might have large underground lakes of water. The tidal pull from Saturn heats Enceladus enough to keep the water liquid.

Much of the ejected water falls back to the surface. But because the water is traveling so fast, some of it leaves Enceladus for good. It then spirals down toward Saturn, where it forms much of Saturn's outermost E ring.

Saturn has another moon that may have cryogeysers. This is Titan, Saturn's largest moon and one of the largest moons in the solar system. Titan is 3,200 miles (5,150 km) in diameter, about 50 percent bigger than Earth's Moon. It is also the only moon in the solar system known to have a real atmosphere. In fact, Titan's atmosphere is denser than Earth's. Like Earth's atmosphere, Titan's is made mostly of nitrogen. There is little or no oxygen, however, so it would be impossible for humans to breathe there.

Titan also has a lot of methane. This is a gas similar to one that is used for cooking. Scientists were never sure where all the methane in Titan's atmosphere was coming from. Some suspected that it might be brought from beneath the surface by erupting cryovolcanoes. Images taken in 2004 by the *Cassini* orbiter revealed such a volcano on the surface.

Instead of lava, the volcano probably erupts water, ammonia, and methane. On Earth these are normally liquid, like water, or a gas, like methane. But Titan's surface is a frigid –290°F (–179°C). At that temperature, water freezes to a solid—ice as hard as steel—and methane is a liquid.

Of all the amazing volcanic wonders of the solar system, Io still tops the list. It may be one of the most dangerous places in the solar system. But history has shown that danger has seldom kept tourists away from viewing so great a wonder.

Scientists think that Saturn's moon Titan might have cryogeysers, as shown in this illustration.

This image of Uranus's moon Miranda was captured by Voyager 2 in 1986. Miranda's surface is very rugged.

$\mathcal{U}$RANUS HAS PERHAPS THE LARGEST COLLECTION OF UNUSUAL MOONS IN THE SOLAR SYSTEM. THERE ARE TWENTY-ONE OF THEM (AT LAST COUNT). THE FIVE LARGEST MOONS WERE DISCOVERED BY ASTRONOMERS BEFORE THE *VOYAGER 2* FLYBY IN 1986. THEY RANGE IN SIZE FROM 293 MILES (472 KM) TO 980 MILES (1,578 KM) IN DIAMETER. MANY MORE MOONS HAVE BEEN DISCOVERED SINCE, INCLUDING SEVERAL BY *VOYAGER 2*.

The innermost of the five large moons, Miranda, was discovered in 1948. It is just 147 miles (236 km) in diameter. Uranus is only 80,782 miles (130,000 km) away from it. On Miranda, Uranus would appear eighty-eight times larger than a full moon looks from here on Earth. It would fill Miranda's sky like an enormous blue balloon.

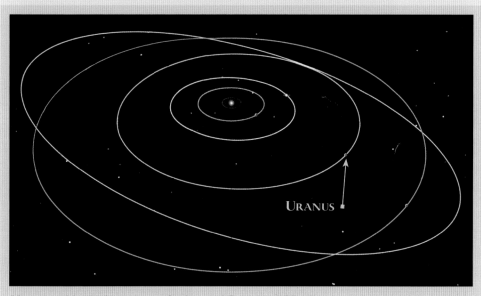

URANUS

Uranus orbits in deep space, far beyond Saturn and Jupiter.

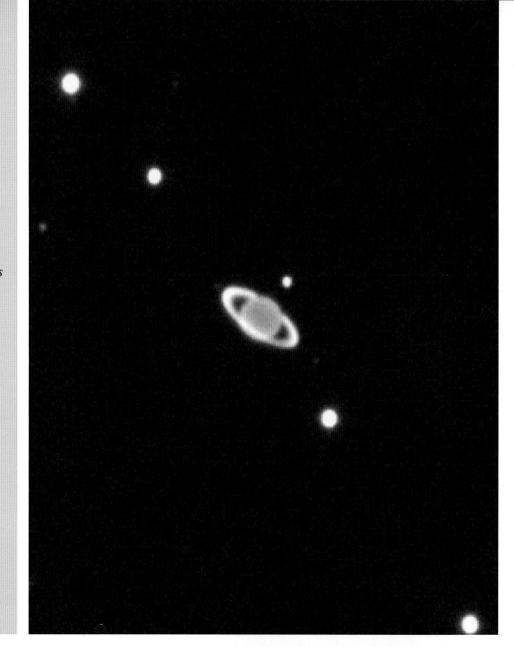

This image shows the rings and several of the moons of Uranus. Miranda is the circle directly above Uranus.

Photos taken by *Voyager 2* reveal Miranda as a world that must have had an extraordinarily violent history. It looks very much as though it had been broken into pieces and put back together any which way. The landscape is a tortured collection of valleys, cracks, grooves, and steep cliffs.

What caused Miranda to look like this? Miranda orbits very close to the Roche limit

MIRANDA *Facts*

Distance from Uranus: 80,642
miles (129,780 km)
Diameter: 292 miles (470 km)
Length of time to orbit
Uranus: 1.4 days

of Uranus. The Roche limit determines how close a large object—such as a moon—can get to a planet before the planet's gravity tears it apart. Saturn's rings, which lie within Saturn's Roche limit may be the remains of a moon that strayed too close to the giant planet. Something like this may have happened to Miranda.

In the distant past, Miranda probably had a very different orbit than it does now. Sometimes the orbit brought it very near Uranus. Sometimes it took it far away. These drastic changes in gravity put a lot of stress on the little moon. This caused ice deep within Miranda to melt. The circulation of this warmed material was probably what caused all the fractures in Miranda's surface. At the present time, Miranda's orbit is much more circular. This means there are fewer stresses on it. So stress no longer causes the heating of Miranda, and it is frozen solid all the way through.

Something else may have added to Miranda's appearance. A giant planet such as Uranus attracts a great many meteoroids (small chunks of rock and metal, ranging in size from a grain of dust to a few feet). It also attracts asteroids (large chunks of rock and metal, sometimes many miles wide). Since Miranda is so close to Uranus, it is more likely to run into one of these asteroids than an outer moon would be. It is possible that one of these asteroids was large enough to literally shatter Miranda into pieces, like a baseball hitting a glass fishbowl. The pieces remained in orbit around Uranus, where they eventually reassembled. Some astronomers have suggested that this may have happened as often as five times during Miranda's past.

Whatever the causes may be, the landscape of tiny Miranda is one of the most amazing in the solar system. There are huge canyons as deep as 12 miles (20 km), winding parallel ridges and valleys, and several high cliffs called scarps.

The Great Wall of Miranda is one of these scarps. It is a smooth wall nearly 3 miles (5 km) high. By comparison, Earth's Grand Canyon in only 1 mile (1.6

"Imagine wandering down the twisting canyons [of Miranda] with the turquoise globe of Uranus overhead and the distant Sun's cold glare hiding tiny Earth."
—William K. Hartmann, American astronomer, 2005

This illustration shows Uranus looming over the Great Wall of Miranda.

km) deep. The cliff of the Great Wall of Miranda is very steep. It was created when two vast blocks of Miranda's crust moved—one up and the other down. The great height of the cliff, combined with the low gravity on Miranda, would mean that a clumsy astronaut falling over the edge would take more than five minutes to reach the bottom.

DISCOVERING URANUS AND ITS MOONS

In 1781 British astronomer William Herschel was doing a routine survey of the stars with his homemade telescope. He made an astonishing discovery. At first Herschel thought he had discovered a new comet. But when he worked out its orbit, he realized that it must be a planet. Most comets have highly elliptical (oval-shaped) orbits that are very different from the nearly circular orbits of the planets. Until then everyone had thought there were just five planets. Mercury, Venus, Mars, Jupiter, and Saturn, along with the Sun and Earth, made seven bodies altogether. This was a magic number that seemed perfect to

British astronomer William Herschel discovered the distant planet of Uranus in the late 1700s. But astronomers didn't gain much more information about the planet until Voyager 2 visited in 1986.

WHAT TO NAME A *New Planet?*

Herschel's discovery of a new planet in 1781 took the world by storm. There was a rush to name the new body. Georgium Sidus (George's Star, named for Britain's King George III) was Herschel's choice. Others wanted to name the planet Herschel (which was certainly not his choice!). German mathematician Johann Bode suggested Uranus (after the Greek god of the sky), and it stuck.

many people (just as today some people think that the number thirteen is unlucky). No one ever thought to look for an eighth planet because no one thought there would be one.

Uranus is far from the Sun and difficult to observe. From Earth, with even the most powerful telescopes, Uranus is only the size of a pinhead. Astronomers couldn't learn much about Uranus other than its size and what it was made of. It is composed mostly of hydrogen with some helium and methane, very much like Neptune, Jupiter, and Saturn are. It wasn't until *Voyager 2* visited in 1986 that astronomers learned more about the planet.

Uranus orbits 1.78 billion miles (2.87 billion km) from the Sun. That is nearly twenty times farther than Earth is from the Sun. This means that nearly four hundred times less sunlight reaches that planet than reaches Earth. Uranus is a large planet, 31,765 miles (51,120 km) in diameter. That is four times the size of Earth. Its surface gravity, though, is only 88 percent that of Earth. This is because Uranus is made mostly of very light materials that do not have much mass. In addition to hydrogen and helium, Uranus has water ice, methane, and ammonia. It has a large rocky core. It takes Uranus eighty-four years to circle the Sun just once. Only two Uranus years have passed since its discovery in 1781.

GIANT SCARPS ON OTHER WORLDS

Other worlds have scarps created in the same way as Miranda's Great Wall. Mercury has several long scarps. These range from 1,000 feet (304 m) to 2 miles (3 km) high and from 10 to more than 300 miles (16 to 484 km) long. Like those on Miranda, these were created when gigantic blocks of Mercury's surface rose above the surrounding area. Earth has scarps like these, where blocks of the crust have moved in different directions. A scarp in California 10 feet (3 m) high was created during the earthquake that destroyed San Francisco in 1906.

One of Jupiter's four large moons, Europa, also has large scarps. Most of them are part of a system of cliffs called Tyre. Because the scarps are arranged in curves, scientists believe Tyre is the result of being hit by an asteroid. This impact caused Europa's thick, icy crust to shatter into huge blocks. It would

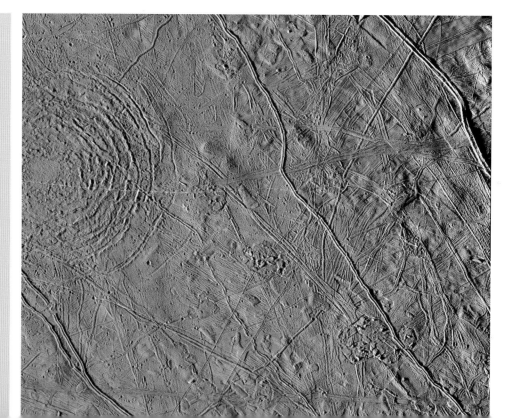

This close-up of Europa's surface shows several large scarps arranged in curves. Europa is one of Jupiter's large moons.

have been like dropping a heavy stone onto a frozen pond. Tyre has a diameter of 2,485 miles (4,000 km), making it one of the largest impact features in the solar system.

Earth's Moon also has a giant scarp. It was first seen in 1686 by the Danish astronomer Christiaan Huygens. It is known as the Straight Wall. Its official name is Rupes Recta, which is Latin for "straight cliff." The scarp stands out because it lies in a flat, smooth plain, and it is almost 75 miles (120 km) long. Estimates of its height range from 820 to 1,300 feet (250 to 400 m). It is a favorite target for amateur astronomers.

THE MYSTERIOUS WALL OF IAPETUS

Iapetus is one of Saturn's smaller moons. It is one of the most interesting bodies in the solar system. Giovanni Domenico Cassini discovered Iapetus in 1671. That was more than three hundred years before anyone saw a close-up photo of the small moon. But even in 1671, astronomers knew there was something unique about the moon. For one thing, its brightness changed as it orbited Saturn. It was twice as bright when it appeared on one side of the planet than on the other side. The only explanation scientists could think of was that half of Iapetus was almost black and the other half almost white. When the dark side was facing Earth, Iapetus looked dim. When the light side was facing Earth, Iapetus looked bright.

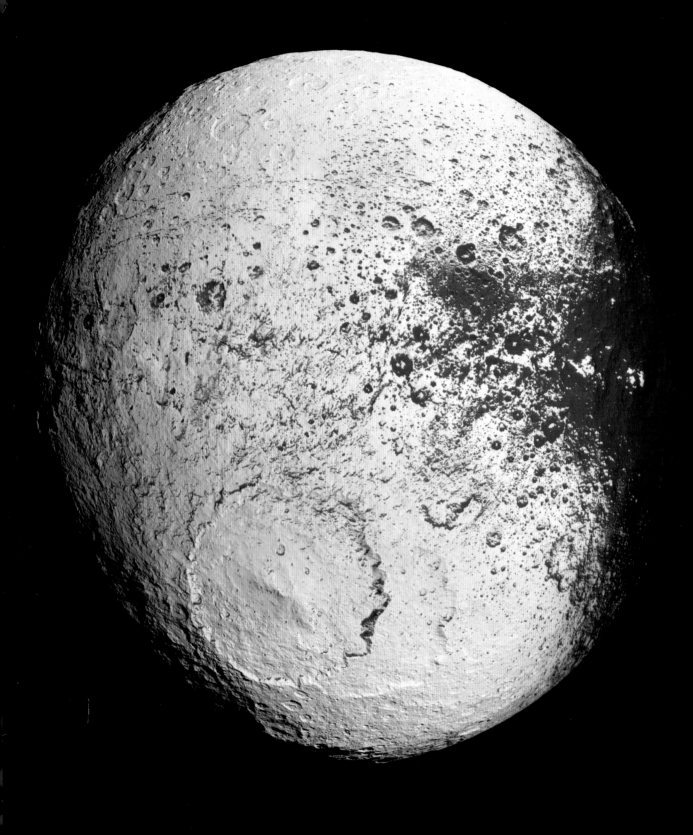

Iapetus—one of Saturn's smaller moons—is half black and half white. This image shows the black part of the moon just beginning to come into view.

This guess proved to be correct. The first photos of Iapetus taken by the spacecraft *Voyager 2* in 1981 revealed that Iapetus was indeed half black and half white. The S-shaped dividing line between the two halves is very sharp. Scientists aren't certain why Iapetus looks this way. Dark material might have been blown off the next outermost moon, Phoebe, by meteor impacts. This material would fall toward Saturn. Since Iapetus is between Phoebe and Saturn, the small moon might have swept up some of this material. But no one is sure.

Another astonishing feature on Iapetus is the mountain range that circles the equator. It is an almost perfect straight line. The ridge makes the moon look something like a walnut. It is as though Iapetus is made of two halves that have been squashed together. The range is at least 800 miles (1,300 km) long. It wraps one-third of the way around the moon. It may even be longer, but astronomers don't know for sure. So far, only part of the surface of Iapetus has been photographed.

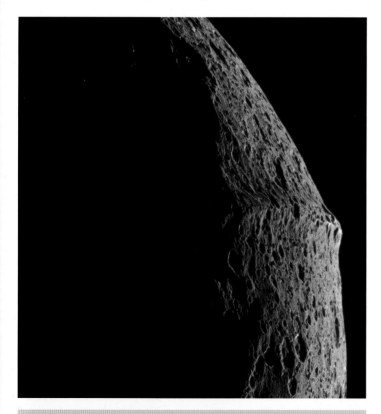

The equatorial mountain range on Iapetus stands up to 8 miles (13 km) above the surrounding surface.

The peaks of the range are up to 8 miles (13 km) high. This is 3 miles (5 km) higher than the highest mountains on Earth. No one knows what formed this mountain range. It may have been created by a fold in the icy crust of the moon. Or it might have been formed by material flowing up through a crack in the surface. It is still a complete mystery.

The solar system is filled with amazing cliffs and strange mountains. But for sheer amazement, few are more impressive than the Great Wall of Miranda.

5 Herschel Crater ON MIMAS

Mimas (above) *is one of at least*
sixty-two moons that orbit Saturn.

$\mathcal{F}$EW CRATERS ARE AS PERFECT OR AS BEAUTIFUL AS THE GIANT ONE ON MIMAS, A MOON OF SATURN. HERSCHEL CRATER WAS CREATED BY AN ASTEROID CRASHING INTO MIMAS. MIMAS WAS ALMOST DESTROYED BY THE IMPACT. THE CRATER LEFT BY THE CRASH IS 81 MILES (130 KM) WIDE. THIS IS ALMOST ONE-THIRD THE SIZE OF THE ENTIRE MOON, WHICH IS ONLY 247 MILES (397 KM) IN DIAMETER. IF EARTH HAD A CRATER AS LARGE IN PROPORTION, IT WOULD BE AS WIDE AS THE UNITED STATES. CRACKS MADE BY THE SHOCK WAVES FROM THE IMPACT CAN BE SEEN ALL THE WAY AROUND MIMAS.

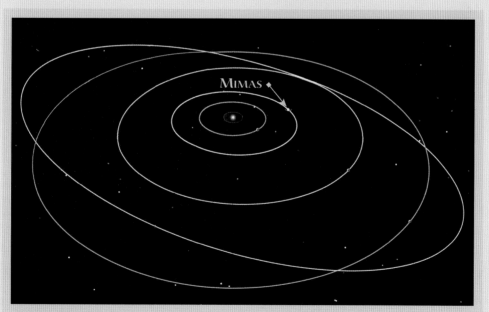

Mimas orbits Saturn below the planet's rings.

If you could stand on the rim of Herschel Crater, the view would be one of the most spectacular in the solar system. The crater walls are 3 miles (5 km) high. They would look like great cliffs curving off into the distance. The floor of the crater would be more than 6 miles (10 km) below your feet. A towering peak in the center of the crater would dominate your view. It is 3.7 miles (6 km) high, almost as high as Mount Everest, the tallest mountain on Earth.

But overwhelming the scene would be Saturn itself. The giant planet is only 115,000 miles (185,520 km) away. This is less than half the distance separating Earth from the Moon. Saturn is so much bigger than Earth's Moon that it would look seventy-five times larger than a full Moon does in the night sky of Earth. It would fill the sky above Herschel Crater.

This illustration shows a close-up view of Herschel Crater on Mimas. Saturn fills the horizon.

The Cassini *spacecraft captured this image of Mimas orbiting Saturn in 2008. Saturn is less than half the distance from Mimas that Earth is from its Moon.*

Every planet and moon in the solar system has been hit by meteors or asteroids—many, many thousands of them. The gas giants don't show any effects of these strikes because they are made of gas and liquid. An asteroid crashing into a planet such as Jupiter or Saturn would no more leave a crater than a stone dropped into a pond would leave a hole in the water. But the solid worlds, those like our own Earth and Moon, have many old scars. Earth has been hit thousands of times in the past. Because it is larger, it has been hit many more times than the Moon. Still it isn't scarred by craters the way the Moon is.

Weather is the main reason for this. Millions of years of wind and rain have eroded all but the very youngest Earth craters. Meteor Crater in Arizona is one of the best preserved. It was formed only about thirty thousand years ago.

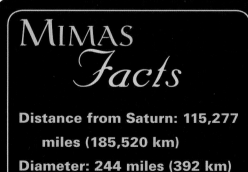

MIMAS *Facts*

Distance from Saturn: 115,277 miles (185,520 km)
Diameter: 244 miles (392 km)
Length of time to orbit Saturn: 0.9 days

"If the crater had been any bigger, Mimas would have been broken into pieces!"
—*William K. Hartmann, American planetary scientist, 2010*

A man gazes over Meteor Crater in Arizona. Like Herschel Crater on Mimas, Meteor Crater on Earth was created by the impact of a meteor.

That's not long enough for lava and ash from volcanoes to replace ancient land with new. But Meteor Crater is not that large. The largest crater on Earth of which there is anything remaining is Vredefort Crater. It is in South Africa and is 186 miles (300 km) wide. It was created two billion years ago when a small asteroid slammed into Earth.

BIG CRATERS ON OTHER WORLDS

Earth's Moon has some enormous craters on it. You can see many of them with an ordinary pair of binoculars. Near the center of the Moon as seen from Earth is a large crater named Copernicus. It is 58

MIMAS AND *the Rings*

One of the most noticeable features of Saturn's rings is the broad gap in it. This gap is called the Cassini Division after the astronomer who discovered it. This gap is created by the little moon Mimas. Particles of ice in the gap would orbit Saturn once for every two orbits that Mimas makes. This means that the gravity of Mimas tugs on these particles on a regular basis. The tug is always in the same direction too. The result is that over time, Mimas has cleared the ring of any particles of ice that might have been in it. Mimas is also responsible for other, smaller gaps in the rings.

miles (93 km) wide. This is about the same size as Yellowstone National Park. Another impressive crater is Tycho. It is a dazzlingly bright spot near the southern edge of the Moon. It was created about 200 million years ago when a small asteroid struck. It left a hole 52 miles (85 km) wide and 3 miles (4.8 km) deep. Bright streamers radiate from the crater. These streamers have been called rays. They were created when material blasted from the crater fell back to the surface.

Below: *This image of craters on the Moon was taken by* Apollo 10 *astronauts in 1969.* Left: *The Tycho crater is the bright white spot at the bottom of this image of the Moon.*

The very largest crater on the Moon is on the side we can't see from Earth. It is the South Pole-Aitken Basin. This crater lies near the south pole of the Moon. It was created 3.9 billion years ago while the Moon was still young. Its enormous hole is 1,550 miles (2,500 km) wide and 8 miles (13 km) deep. It is the second-largest impact feature in the entire solar system—and the deepest one. Since the Moon itself is only 2,159 miles (3,475 km) wide, you can get some idea of how big this impact must have been. The asteroid that created the basin punched a hole so deep into the Moon that molten lava poured out onto the surface. This filled most of the basin. It created the broad flat plane of smooth rock.

This illustration shows how the South Pole-Aitken Basin might have been created millions of years ago when an asteroid collided with the Moon. Earth is in the bottom left corner.

TINY WORLDS, *Giant Craters*

Some of the smaller worlds also have impressive craters. These craters are not nearly as large as those on Mars or the Moon. If the world is small, however, the crater can be huge in comparison. Mars has two tiny moons. One of them, Phobos *(below)*, is a potato-shaped rock measuring only 17 by 14 by 11 miles (27 by 22 by 18 km). It has a crater (called Stickney) 5.6 miles (9 km) in diameter. The impact that created the crater nearly split Phobos in half. Proof of this lies in the hundreds of cracks that cover the surface of this small moon.

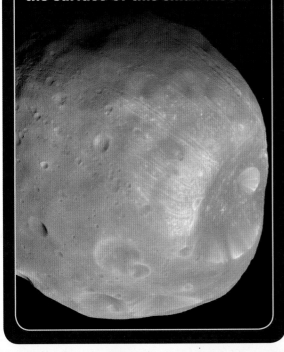

The largest crater in the entire solar system is on Mars. Called the Borealis Basin, it covers about 40 percent of the surface of Mars. This crater is 5,300 miles (8,500 km) wide. This equals the distance between Los Angeles, California, and London, England. Borealis is about four times wider than the third-biggest impact basin known. This is the Hellas Basin, which is also on Mars. The object that crashed into Mars would have been about 1,200 miles (2,000 km) across. That would make it larger than Pluto.

Every world in the solar system—except for the gas giants—can boast of at least one giant crater. But few possess one as beautiful or as impressive as Herschel Crater on Mimas.

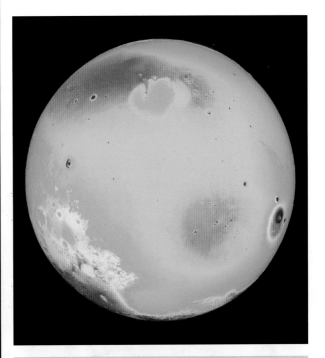

This image of the north pole of Mars uses colors to show elevation. The blue area is the Borealis Basin, which covers 40 percent of the planet.

This picture combines two images of Jupiter to show the auroras (glowing lights) that occur at the poles.

$\mathcal{M}$ANY OF THE PLANETS OF THE SOLAR SYSTEM ARE LIKE MAGNETS. THE CORES AT THE CENTER OF THESE PLANETS—WHICH ARE MADE MOSTLY OF METAL—CREATE POWERFUL MAGNETIC FIELDS. EARTH IS ONE OF THESE PLANETS. ITS MAGNETIC FIELD IS WHAT CAUSES A COMPASS NEEDLE TO POINT NORTH.

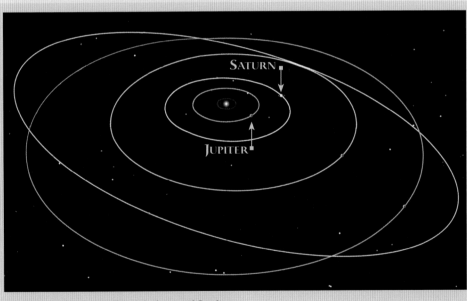

Saturn's orbit (in yellow) is beyond Jupiter.

Earth's magnetic field also attracts electrical particles emitted from the Sun. These particles constantly flow from the Sun in a stream called the solar wind. Solar wind particles strike the atmosphere high above the North Pole and the South Pole. When the electrical particles strike the gas molecules that make up Earth's atmosphere they cause the gases to glow. (The same thing happens in a neon sign. Electricity causes the gas in the glass tube to glow.) We can often see this bright glow in the atmosphere. In the northern sky, it is called the aurora borealis. In the south, it is called the aurora australis. These

THE COLORS OF
Auroras

Each different gas in the atmosphere of a planet glows in different colors. These colors tell which gas is being affected by the electrical energy of the Sun. On Earth the most common color seen (and usually the brightest one) is the yellow green produced by oxygen atoms. This occurs at a low altitude of about 60 miles (97 km). Oxygen at higher altitudes (200 miles, or 320 km) creates a red glow. Electrically charged nitrogen produces blue light. Electrically neutral nitrogen produces a purple red aurora.

The aurora borealis, or northern lights, trails across the sky above Denali National Park in Alaska.

names mean northern lights and southern lights, respectively. From space an aurora looks like a ring of light circling a planet's polar region.

THE AURORAS OF SATURN

Saturn has spectacular auroras that circle the poles like flaming crowns. Just as on Earth, particles from the solar wind pour onto Saturn's poles. When these particles collide with the gases in Saturn's atmosphere, they glow. But Saturn is a much larger world than Earth. Saturn has a much more powerful magnetic field. So it attracts the solar wind much more strongly to create incredible displays of glowing patterns of light.

"We've never seen an aurora like this elsewhere . . . finding such a bright one [on Saturn] is a fantastic surprise."
—*Tom Stallard, astronomer, University of Leicester, Great Britain, 2008*

Above: *The bright auroras on Saturn can last for days.*

Right: *The Hubble Telescope captured this image of both of Saturn's auroras in 2009. Because of Saturn's orbit, the opportunity to see both poles at once occurs only once every fifteen years.*

Below: *This illustration represents what the auroras on Saturn might look like from the planet itself.*

> *"It's not just a ring of auroras like those we've seen at Jupiter or Earth. This aurora covers an enormous area across the pole."*
>
> —Tom Stallard, astronomer, University of Leicester, Great Britain, 2008

Saturn's auroras are long lasting too. An aurora on Earth might last only ten minutes. Saturn's auroras can last for many days. Measurements made by the *Cassini* spacecraft show that the auroras move with Saturn as it spins on its axis. But images from the Hubble Space Telescope show that sometimes the auroras remain still while the planet rotates beneath them. Scientists aren't certain why this happens.

JUPITER'S AURORAS

Jupiter also has auroras at its poles. Like Saturn, Jupiter has a much more powerful magnetic field than Earth. Jupiter's rapid rotation—once every ten hours—causes its magnetic field to generate a million megawatts of power

AURORAS ON *Other Worlds*

Auroras are usually associated with planets with strong magnetic fields. But they have been observed on other planets and even some moons. Faint auroras have been detected on Venus and Mars, for instance. In addition to the spectacular auroras on Jupiter's moon, Io, auroras have also been seen on Europa and Ganymede.

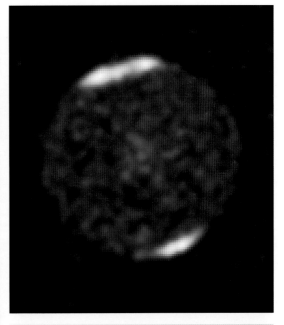

This X-ray of Jupiter shows the X-ray emissions associated with auroras at Jupiter's poles.

around the poles. This is ten times the power generated by Earth's auroras. This would be enough all by itself to create a beautiful light show. But unlike Earth and Saturn, Jupiter doesn't depend on the solar wind to create its auroras. It provides plenty of energy all on its own.

Charged particles from the moon Io also flood onto the poles. These particles are similar to the ones in the solar wind. They come from the dozens of volcanoes that are constantly erupting on Io's surface. Io throws more than one ton (1 metric ton) of this material into space every second. A kind of electrical connection exists between Jupiter and Io. Energy constantly flows between the two of them. This stream of energy is called the Io flux tube. It

This diagram shows Io's flux tube (stream of energy) and how the sulfur from Io's volcanoes makes its way to Jupiter's auroras.

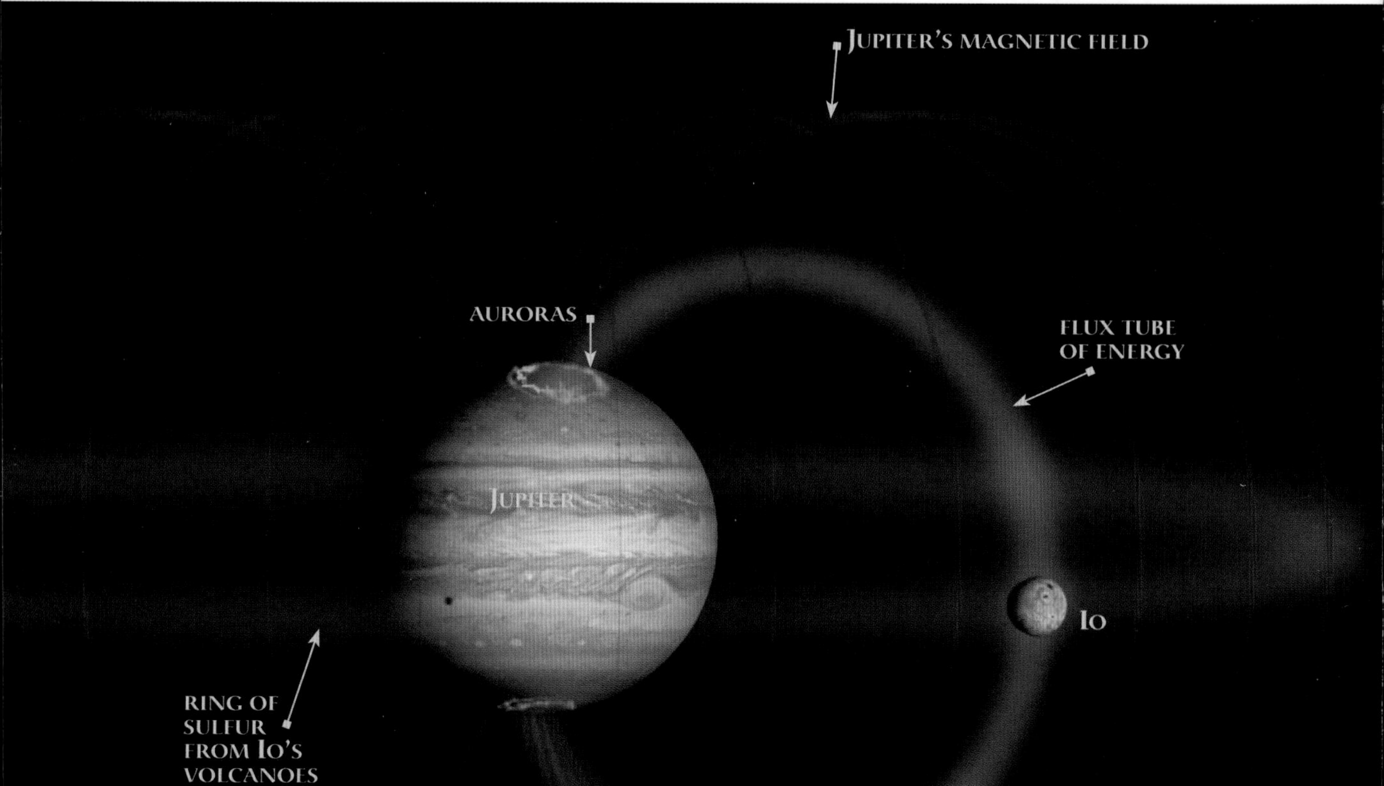

JUPITER'S MAGNETIC FIELD

AURORAS

FLUX TUBE OF ENERGY

JUPITER

Io

RING OF SULFUR FROM Io'S VOLCANOES

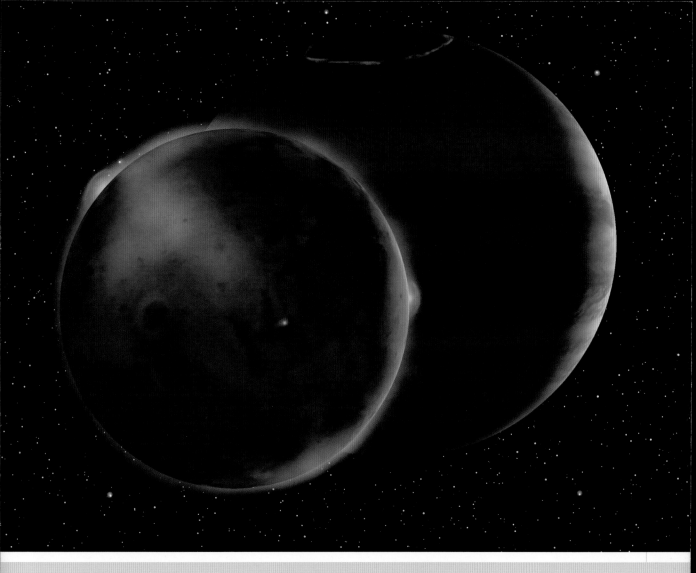

The electrical connection between Io and Jupiter causes Io to have auroras. This illustration shows auroras on both the planet and its moon. Io looks large because it is closer to the viewer.

is like a loop of wire connecting Jupiter and Io. Jupiter's auroras are strongest where the ends of the flux tube connect with the planet. The result is that Jupiter's auroras are affected much more by Io than by the solar wind. Jupiter's spectacular auroras are larger than the entire Earth.

Even Io itself has auroras. Its electrical connection with Jupiter works both ways. The result is that the night sky of Io—filled with gases from its volcanoes— is full of glowing clouds of multicolored light.

For all the wonder and beauty of the auroras of Earth, Jupiter, and Io, however, none can compare with the lights in the sky of Saturn.

7 THE UNDERGROUND SEA of Europa

This illustration imagines what it would be like to view Europa's ocean from underneath its icy covering.

$\mathcal{E}$ARTH IS THE ONLY PLANET IN THE SOLAR SYSTEM KNOWN TO POSSESS OPEN BODIES OF LIQUID WATER. THREE-QUARTERS OF EARTH IS COVERED IN WATER. UNTIL RECENTLY, SCIENTISTS THOUGHT THAT EARTH WAS THE ONLY BODY IN THE SOLAR SYSTEM TO HAVE AN OCEAN OF LIQUID WATER. BUT ONE OF JUPITER'S MOONS, EUROPA, MAY HAVE AN OCEAN TOO.

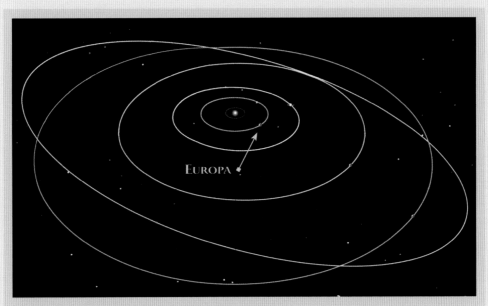

EUROPA

Europa is the smallest of Jupiter's Galilean moons.

Europa lies 249,000 miles (400,000 km) from Jupiter. It is the smallest of the Galilean satellites and one of the strangest-looking moons in the solar system. Photos taken by the *Voyager* spacecraft in 1979 revealed that Europa has almost no craters. Instead, its surface is covered entirely with patterns of overlapping cracks, folds, ridges, and grooves. None of these features rise very far above the surface. Europa's surface resembles a cracked pool ball more than anything else.

All of this would seem to show that Europa's surface is very young. Some forces are constantly renewing the surface. These forces destroy surface features before they can become very old. Europa's smooth surface resembles the ice floes of the Arctic and Antarctic regions of Earth.

ICY EUROPA

The only way to explain these features was if the surface of Europa might in fact be a thick layer of ice floating above an ocean of liquid water. It is the movement of this ice that causes the ridges and grooves to form. Water flowing up through cracks in the surface freezes, creating a new, fresh surface. The top layer of Europa is being constantly re-created.

Europa has no large craters or high mountains because ice is not as hard as rock. It will flow under its own weight. This happens with the ice in glaciers on Earth. The weight of the ice in a glacier will cause it to flow downhill. For the same reason, a crater or mountain on Europa will slowly flatten out.

The ocean that lies beneath the crust of Europa may be as deep as 30 miles (50 km). The water is kept liquid by the nearness of Europa to Jupiter. Tidal forces from the huge planet constantly flex the moon. The tidal flexing of Europa's crust warms the water beneath its surface. This warmth keeps it liquid. Because life as we know it requires liquid water to exist, Europa might be a good candidate in the search for life beyond Earth.

"We do not have definitive evidence for the existence of a liquid ocean, but the information we do have is compelling."

—Ronald Greeley, planetary geologist, 2009

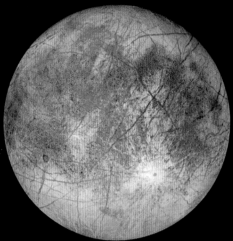

Top left: *Three-quarters of Earth is covered with water.*

Top right: *Europa is covered with ice. The dark brown areas are rocky material.*

Below left: *The surface of Europa resembles the ice floes of Earth's polar regions.*

Below right: *This illustration shows a cutaway of Europa's surface.*

ICY CRUST

ORGANIC MOLECULES

LIQUID WATER OCEAN

WATER CIRCULATION

HEAT FROM BELOW THE SURFACE

One reason scientists think life on Europa might be possible is that colors appear around the cracks in Europa's ice. When underground water erupts from the cracks, it carries colorful compounds with it. These compounds have tinted the ice yellow, pink, orange, and brown. Scientists know that these are the colors of many organic compounds. And where there are organic compounds, life might have evolved.

Scientists hope to land a probe on Europa in the near future. The probe will drill or melt its way through the thick ice crust. A second probe will then be dropped into the ocean beneath. It will be like a tiny robot submarine. It will carry instruments and cameras that might discover the first living organisms beyond Earth.

THE HIDDEN SEAS OF ENCELADUS AND MARS

Smaller versions of Europa's underground ocean may exist on Saturn's moon, Enceladus. The giant plumes of ice crystals that erupt from cracks at its south pole may come from small lakes of liquid water hidden deep

Left: *Enceladus may also have an underground ocean.*
Right: *Jets of ice particles erupt from Enceladus.*

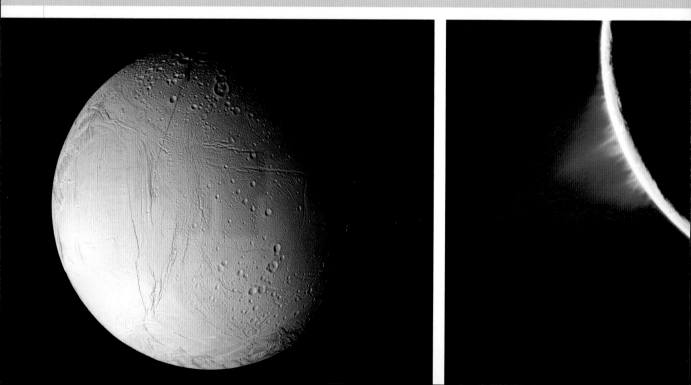

Left: *This image shows an arctic landscape on Earth shaped by permafrost (permanently frozen soil).*

Right: *This image shows the arctic plains of Mars. Both the Earth and the Martian arctics have earth in polygon (multisided) patterns. This indicates repeated freezing and thawing.*

beneath the surface. Like Europa, warmth from tidal flexing keeps the water liquid.

Mars, too, may have vast amounts of water hidden beneath its surface. Much of this is in the form of permafrost. On Earth permafrost is a layer of permanently frozen soil anywhere from 2 to 12 feet (0.6 to 4 m) thick. It covers vast areas of Alaska and northern Canada. In Siberia the permafrost can be thousands of feet thick. Permafrost on Mars may be up to 0.6 to 2 miles (1 to 3 km) thick.

In 2005 the European Space Agency's orbiter *Mars Express* discovered a large frozen lake on Mars. It is buried under a thick layer of volcanic ash. The lake is about 500 by 560 miles (800 by 900 km) in area and about 150 feet (45 m) deep. This is about the same size as the North Sea on Earth. Until recently, most scientists had thought that ice on Mars would to be buried underground as deep as 650 to nearly 1,500 feet (200 to 450 m). At the poles, it might lie only 300 feet (100 m) beneath the surface. But measurements made by NASA's Mars orbiter in 2002 revealed areas where the ice was buried only a few yards down. No one knows how thick this layer of ice might be. It could be thousands of feet or even many miles thick.

This illustration shows a methane lake on Titan.

SEAS OF
Rocket Fuel

Saturn's giant moon, Titan, also has seas hidden beneath the thick orange clouds that cover the moon. Until the *Cassini* spacecraft arrived in 2005, no one had any idea what was beneath Titan's clouds. *Cassini*, however, carried special instruments that could penetrate Titan's cloud cover. They discovered mountains, plains, and narrow winding features that look exactly like rivers and many large lakes.

These lakes are not filled with water. Titan is much too cold for liquid water to exist. Titan's atmosphere is mostly nitrogen with some argon, methane, and tiny amounts of other organic compounds. Liquid methane and ethane may occasionally fall from the clouds in the form of rain. This rain would flow along the river channels to eventually fill the lakes with a slushy liquid of methane and ethane. These could be used as rocket fuel. Both are the main ingredients of natural gas used on Earth to power electric generators, supply heat, and to fuel stoves and ovens. Methane and ethane need oxygen to burn, and Titan has no free oxygen in its atmosphere. But if a spaceship carried its own oxygen, it could refill its fuel tanks from one of Titan's lakes. Since weight is everything in space travel, this means future explorers would only have to take along enough fuel to get to Titan. Their spaceship would then be smaller, lighter, and less expensive than one that had to carry fuel for a round-trip.

The Phoenix *lander took this self-portrait while it scooped samples from the Martian surface in 2008.*

The *Phoenix* lander touched down in the north polar regions of Mars in 2008. One of the first things it did was to scoop away the surface layer of dirt to see what might lie beneath. To the surprise of many scientists, a patch of white was revealed only a few inches under the surface. It was water ice. No one had expected to find ice so close to the surface.

The discovery that water is common on the sister worlds of Earth is one of the most important of this century. And of all these worlds, the one whose oceans most rival Earth's is Europa. Someday tourists may be exploring the sea that lies beneath its ice, marveling at the wonders they see there.

TIMELINE

1610 Galileo Galilei makes the first telescopic observations of Jupiter and Saturn. He is the first to see the four largest moons of Jupiter.

1655 Christiaan Huygens describes the rings of Saturn as a disk surrounding the planet.

1665 Giovanni Domenico Cassini discovers the Great Red Spot on Jupiter.

1675 Cassini discovers the gaps in Saturn's rings. The largest one is named for him.

1781 William Herschel discovers Uranus on March 13.

1846 On September 23, Urbain Le Verrier and John Couch Adams officially discover Neptune.

1972 On March 3, *Pioneer 10* is the first spacecraft to fly by Jupiter.

1973 *Pioneer 11* flies by Jupiter and Saturn.

1977 *Voyager 2* flies by Jupiter and Saturn and makes the first flybys of Uranus and Neptune. *Voyager 1* flies by Jupiter and Saturn.

1979 On March 8, *Voyager 1* takes the first photos of Io's volcanoes.

1989 *Galileo* is the first spacecraft to orbit Jupiter. It also launches a probe into Jupiter's atmosphere.

1990 *Ulysses* spacecraft makes a flyby of Jupiter on October 6.

1997 *Cassini*, the first Saturn orbiter, is launched on October 15.

2004 On July 1, *Cassini* goes into orbit around Saturn.

2005 *Huygens*, a probe carried by *Cassini*, makes the first landing on Titan—a moon of Saturn—on January 14. In November, *Cassini* scientists discover that one of Saturn's moons, Rhea, may have a faint ring system, the first satellite known to have rings. Scientists also discovered giant geysers on another satellite, Enceladus.

2006 *Cassini* discovers lakes of liquid methane on Titan on July 21.

2008 *Cassini* scientists observed water vapor ejected from the surface of Enceladus—a moon of Saturn. On March 12, *Cassini* discovers chemicals in the cryogeysers of Enceladus that suggest conditions may be suitable for life under the surface of this moon.

2009 In June, *Cassini* discovers that the rings of Saturn contain hills, waves, and bumps.

2010 *Cassini* sends back photos from its closest approach to Mimas (a moon of Saturn) on February 15.

CHOOSE AN EIGHTH WONDER

The gas giants and their moons are full of wonderful sights and amazing places—and more are being discovered all the time. There are many candidates for possible future wonders of the solar system's gas giants and their mysterious moons. The solar system is filled with wonderful, amazing places. Do some research on your own or with a friend. See if you can discover some candidates for the eighth wonder of the gas giants and their moons.

To start your research, look through some of the books in the reading list or visit some of the websites. You will find hundreds of wonderful photos of amazing places on these planets. Look for wonders that
- *Have recently been discovered*
- *Show evidence of water on their moons*
- *Are new examples of bodies with rings*

You might even try gathering photos and writing your own chapter on the eighth wonder. Scientists are making amazing new discoveries on the gas giants and their moons all the time. Maybe you will be the scientist who finds the most amazing wonder of all.

GLOSSARY AND PRONUNCIATION GUIDE

asteroid: one of many small bodies composed of rock and metal that orbit the Sun mainly between the orbits of Mars and Jupiter

aurora: a glowing effect in the upper atmosphere of planets caused by electrical particles from the Sun striking molecules of gas in the air

caldera: a large, flat-floored crater caused when land over a lava chamber sinks

crepe ring: the innermost, almost transparent ring of Saturn

crust: the solid outer surface of a planet or satellite

cyclonic storm: any storm that spins in a circle. Hurricanes and tornadoes are cyclonic storms.

Enceladus (en-SEL-uh-duhs): one of the moons of Saturn

fault: a crack in the crust of a planet or a moon caused by the land on either side moving in opposite directions, either parallel to the fault or up and down

geyser: an eruption of steam and liquid created when underground water or some other liquid is heated past the boiling point

helium: a gas. It is the second-lightest element in the universe.

hydrogen: the lightest and most abundant element in the universe

Iapetus (eye-AP-i-tuhs): one of the moons of Saturn

Io (EYE-oh): one of the moons of Jupiter

methane: a colorless, odorless gas that can be used as a fuel

Mimas (MY-muhs): one of the moons of Saturn

nitrogen: a gaseous element that forms 78 percent of Earth's atmosphere

organic molecule: a chemical compound that contains carbon, the basis of life

permafrost: permanently frozen soil. On Earth it is found throughout the polar regions.

scarp: a cliff formed when part of the crust of a planet or a moon moves up or down along a crack called a fault

solar wind: a stream of electrical particles that constantly flows into space from the Sun

SOURCE NOTES

12 A. F. O'D. Alexander, *The Planet Saturn* (New York: Dover Publications, 1962), 85.

14 Mark Russell, "Mark Russell Quotes," ThinkExist.com, 2009, http://thinkexist.com/quotes/mark_russell/ (December 1, 2009).

16 Carolyn Porco, "Carolyn Porco," ThinkExist.com, 2009, http://thinkexist.com/quotes/carolyn_porco/2.html (December 1, 2009).

17 Edward Weiler, quoted in Leonard David, "Ring Around the Planet: Cassini's First Images of Saturn from Orbit," Space.com, July 1, 2004, http://www.space.com/scienceastronomy/cassini_rings_040701.html (December 1, 2009).

23 *Philosophical Transactions of the Royal Society* 1, no. 3 (1664), 4.

34 Linda Morabito Kelly, "The Stories Behind the Mission: Linda Morabito Kelly," Planetary Society, 2002, http://www.planetary.org/explore/topics/space_missions/voyager/stories_kelly.html (December 1, 2009).

35 Ibid.

39 Rosaly Lopes, quoted in NASA/Jet Propulsion Laboratory, "Titan's Volcanoes Give NASA Spacecraft Chilly Reception," ScienceDaily, December 16, 2008, http://www.sciencedaily.com/releases/2008/12/081215194108.htm (December 1, 2009).

43 William K. Hartmann, in Ron Miller and William K. Hartmann, The Grand Tour (New York: Workman, 2005), 213.

53 William K. Hartmann, personal correspondence with author, January 6, 2010.

61 Tom Stallard, quoted in Imaginova Corp., "Dazzling Mysteries Aurora Spotted on Saturn," Fox News, 2008, http://www.foxnews.com/story/0,2933,451372,00.html (December 1, 2009).

63 Tom Stallard, quoted in "Cassini Finds Mysterious New Aurora on Saturn," NASA, 2008, http://www.nasa.gov/mission_pages/cassini/media/cassini-20081112.html (April 30, 2010).

68 Ronald Greeley, quoted in Irene Klotz, "Europa, Jupiter's Moon, Could Support Complex Life," Discovery News, October 8, 2009, http://news.discovery.com/space/europa-ocean-oxygen-life.html (April 30, 2010).

SELECTED BIBLIOGRAPHY

Beatty, J. Kelly, Carolyn Collins Petersen, and Andrew Chaikin, eds. *The New Solar System.* Cambridge, MA: Sky Publishing Corp., 1999.

Faure, Gunter, and Teresa Mensing. *Introduction to Planetary Science.* Dordrecht, The Netherlands: Springer, 2007.

Hartmann, William K. *Moons and Planets.* Belmont, CA: Wadsworth Publishing Co., 1999.

Hunt, Garry, and Patrick Moore. *Jupiter.* New York: Rand McNally, 1981.

Miller, Ron, and William K. Hartmann. *The Grand Tour.* New York: Workman, 2005.

FURTHER READING AND WEBSITES

Books

Butts, Ellen R, and Joyce R.. Schwartz. *Carl Sagan*. Minneapolis: Twenty-First Century Books, 2001. Learn more about the American astronomer Carl Sagan in this biography.

Farndon, John. *Exploring the Solar System*. Portsmouth, NH: Heinemann, 2009. Case studies and profiles of scientists and their research can be found here.

Kopps, Steven. *Killer Rocks from Outer Space*. Minneapolis: Twenty-First Century Books, 2004. The author describes the many objects hurtling through the universe.

Lovett, Laura, Joan Horvath, Jeff Cuzzi, and Kim Stanley Robinson. *Saturn: A New View*. New York: Abrams, 2006. This book contains a collection of 150 of the best photos taken by the *Cassini* spacecraft.

MacLachlan, James. *Galileo*. New York: Oxford University Press, 1997. This book is a good biography of the great scientist written for younger readers.

Silverstein, Alvin, Virginia Silverstein, and Laura Silverstein Nunn. *Plate Tectonics*. Minneapolis: Twenty-First Century Books, 2009. This book explains the theory of plate tectonics and how moving plates can cause huge changes.

——. *The Universe*. Minneapolis: Twenty-First Century Books, 2009. This book explores the planets of the solar system and worlds beyond.

Spangenburg, Ray, and Kit Moser. *A Look at Jupiter*. Chicago: Children's Press. 2002. The authors provide an introduction to Jupiter and its many moons.

Websites

Astronomy
http://www.astronomy.com
This is the official website for *Astronomy* magazine.

Cassini
http://saturn.jpl.nasa.gov/
This is the official NASA site for the Cassini-Huygens mission to Saturn.

Ciclops Cassini Imaging
http://ciclops.org/
The site is the official source for images from the *Cassini* orbiter studying Saturn.

Galileo
http://galileo.jpl.nasa.gov/
The is the official NASA site for the *Galileo* mission to Jupiter.

Nine Planets
http://www.nineplanets.org/
This is a website filled with information and photos about the planets and their moons.

Sky & Telescope
http://www.skypub.com
This is the official website for *Sky & Telescope* magazine.

INDEX

ABOUT THE AUTHOR

Hugo Award–winning author and illustrator Ron Miller specializes in books about science. Among his various titles, he has written *The Elements: What You Really Want to Know, Special Effects: An Introduction to Movie Magic,* and *Digital Art: Painting with Pixels.* His favorite subjects are space and astronomy. A postage stamp he created is currently on board a spaceship headed for Pluto. His original paintings can be found in collections all over the world. Miller lives in Virginia.